The Language of Myrrh

James S Welch

Dedication

If you feel trapped in silence, bound by pain, and are searching for a language of your own; these words are dedicated to you.

Contents

A Note From the Author

The first poem is addressed to my abuser. The subsequent pieces can be read as a conversation between my deepest heart and God.

The true effectiveness of these poems lie in reading them aloud. Breath can release the turmoil locked within the soul, so inhale and read, exhale and release.

Each section has undertones of what day-part represent: morning, afternoon, and evening. Our hearts are designed to enter different rooms of revelation that are more accessible during different parts of the day. I would encourage you to reflect upon the rich harvest you encounter as you walk through your day, breathing these poems. There are also blank spaces provided to allow you to respond in your own words; kernels

of reflection or wisdom-nuggets coming
to the surface as you journey forward.

Strength and courage will protect you
as you continue on.

(You) Never Heard My No

When you scooped my soul
And drank your fill
When my head kissed the windowsill
Then you slept
And I slipped to the bedroom floor
Escaping the cage
Your words and your rage

I made the carpet my pillow
Turned my face to the wall
Where dust bunnies and monsters all
Saw bruises I tried to never show

In so many desperate ways
Within a battered haze
-I called above, around, beyond, below-
I spoke so clearly the letters
But you never heard my NO.

A reservoir of resin

Embraced by a living tree of myrrh

Nurtured earth touching heaven

So growing wholeness can occur

Morning

13

The Wells of the Wind

Gather your hopes

Open your heart to the dawn

far past the unfolding twigs of a moment

Our feathers, woven with rest

Free from fears long gone

Are dipped in the wells of the wind

Where strength that lasts is drawn

Take flight

Our soaring cry

Thunders like a growing storm

Abandoned to the vaults of this endless sky

Our confining nest no longer belongs

September's Dawn

In sovereign skies of hope
So many stars like candles burning
The oil of my altar ascends like a song returning

Hope hidden in the skies
Where winds are ribbons streaming
Wrapped in wonder I entertain Wisdom's dreaming

Like fingers kneading my hope
Rolling out my cautious light
Sovereign and ancient, Wisdom guides my flight

My heart has wings in the front
Which joyously open in surprise
When Wisdom follows me into the windy skies

A kingdom transformation begins to unfold
The mysteries within are glorious to behold
For my name is a story waiting to be told

I Saw the Face of the Wind

I heard its song from the cleft of a stone
Its eyes held dreams like gold
Reflecting a future for me alone

Waves like crashing diamonds
Drew over my heart with a laugh
In swirling shadows I walked
Beside Wisdom upon an ancient path

Wings of flame flashed in the sky beyond
Turbulent winters crowded below
Thunders peeled open the depths of the sea
Until stillness returned with treasures of snow

Curtains of light dance upon the shore
Wind weaving an infinite tapestry
Plunge with me into the depths of mystery
And be clothed with rivers of eternity

Job 28

I have crept beneath the mountain

To hear the whispers of Job.

Stirred by ornate wonder

Kept within this gilded abode

I step from pathways to sunken shafts

Plummeting spiraling depths

Toward the veins of silver fountains

And guarded mysteries Wisdom protects

Feathers stir somewhere

Far overhead; free from foil or snare

Where the wind sighs

I was there

Near the granite skies

By some miracle the sunlight shines
Dwindling down into the uprooted
sediment

Distilled, flickering like gold in the air
Overseeing the carven halls
Yet recalling the turquoise skies

Breathing in the light
I pause but do not linger long
Burrowing toward the fountain
Where Wisdom hides with Him
Who commands the dawn

At the top of my pockets are clods of brokenness
Crumbling instances of unplanned openness
Yet I've come to trade for treasure
Yearning to grasp that luminous display
Revealed in the grace of God's pleasure
Hope guiding this determined foray
So stillness becomes my garment of peace

Eyes open and hands eager
To fill my heart with sapphires of trust
Rubies flower like fiery curtains
Every word from Wisdom
Laden with golden dust

Within these buried towers
The burden of joy is pleasing and fair
And in all of my future endeavors
I pray I never come away from there

Become a New Person

Become myself

Who I am today

Is good enough

-and that's ok.

I am full; I am whole

Re-collecting all my pieces

All the parts I've left along the way

Even when I fly into frustration

All of me is more than ok.

Through Christ I am made new!

I am myself: pure, complete, and true.

To Find My Place in the Kingdom

I wonder

Bringing my Mountain

I'm under

If a thousand countries

Are my portion in store

Govern to bring those gates through

The Door

Fear of the Lord is the beginning

Of walking with Wisdom

We wander down that path

Bringing our countries with us

We speak with the voice of men and angels

And now I teach them love

God turned His back towards Moses

To take us into His arms before the beginning

Behind the fire

Incense and worship rise

Apple blossoms of your heart

Form reflections in His eyes

With bright wonder

And brass exclamations

The trumpets of prolonged hope

Decorate the arrival of justice

Afternoon

31

Grain

The grain is here
Lintel and mantle
Through the Door
Kernel and seed

Drift into harvest
Thresholds laugh
Part wheat and chaff
Lift the journey

Germinate identity
Wear your mantle
Words are heaven-dew
Your stories honey-sweet

Hear, the answer calls
Seasons of stillness
Open gates
Break glass walls

Restore unity

Clasp hands

Joy-fruit shared

Surrounds the mantles we wear

Ruth (Part 1)

My name is Ruth
And I heard a sound
Of harvest-grain
Falling to the ground
From there rose a soft ascension
Of the warm harvest wheat
Across the threshold to the threshing floor
Transformation complete

I gleaned those that thought they were passed over
Saved for later doesn't mean rejected
In the right season you'll return
Ripe, equipped, whole, and protected
Husk and chaff

Separated

Every kernel with hope for something more
Beyond the lintel and through the door

Gather in the doorway of joy

And brace yourself beneath its beams

Across the threshold to the threshing floor

Beyond the lintel and through the door

Prepare to harvest your faith

Gleaming hope like never before

What Are Graves

To me?

But places to come up from

Yet I catch myself hiding

In the clothes I wore when I slept

In the depths of my voluntary coffins

Mud-mixed ash clings upon my heart

I let my eyes cavitate in

But they should be flowing out...

Light

Light and life

All the places in my being

No boulders belong on my words

Stones thrown in anger

But feathers should fall from my lips

Flakes of gold and silver dust

If I am round with smooth edges

I fit further into eternity

And escape the snare of the grave's flame.

So Here's How It Is:

Movement is necessary

Don't mistake peace for static entropy

Growth is constant

To be still is to grow roots

To move forward is to rise up

Break bread and gain strength

It continues: knitting and unknitting

The very fabric of your DNA

Layers fold and gather together

Stretch and renew

If the waters of your soul become stagnant

Go back and look at the River again

Water falls from great heights

Do not settle for complacency!

In a whirlwind we fly

Until we find the eye

Then we launch further into the sky

Higher and higher toward storm and fire

It's upward and onward we run and run

We've only just begun

Do I seek revenge

   For my trauma?

      Wrapped in the velvet cloth

         Of a labeled experience

And delivered with all the knives

   Of counterfeit justice?

      Take a breath.

I choose to know

   And validate

      My hurt.

I Pull Light

Into my wounds
And sprinkle freedom over my past
So I can be restored
To me again:

With crown of dust
My head lifting
Breathing crust
The bread of mud
My heart softly sifting
I taste gold
From the silt of night grasping dawn

Eyes filled with trust
Like a song lilting
Clean, free of dust
Dread and blood beyond the grave tilting
I bid fear at last be gone
Light, and deep-like flight
Gather both and begin to journey on

Ruth (Part 2)

Traveling from earth to sky
Like Jacob you are a ladder
Linked to the sea of glass
Where angels gather
To see what will come to pass
They ascend and descend
On the sound of your heart
The gates of your soul going up
And your spirit coming down
Revelation pouring in
And the kingdom pouring out

The core of you is sealed in hope
Beauty reflecting from side to side
Your gates go ever higher
Lift your head and keep your heart open wide
Grace and joyous strength flows
Within a righteous tide
Bountiful justice and mercy
Guiding the course of every stride

Now behold the determined harvesters

Who burn and smell like praise

Their eyes are lit with love

And they move in supernatural ways

I am Ruth

I stand in the frame

Go beyond the door

Into the sound of His name

Joy Breathes

Crumpled wrappers
And collapsing paper cups
Soggy steps up a concrete stairway

Mud like coffee grounds
Scraped from my mind
Onto the welcome mat
I though I left yesterday
Behind me in the rain

Tend to the unraveling fray
-The streams-
That bedraggle my mind
Weave skillful colors
Into each harshest hurt
Collect the threads
To blanket grace over all
And let joy breathe with pain...

Cramped like a question
Fit into too small an answer:
My wounds were worse
When asked to live unheard;
Poetry amplifies the music
hiding in the silence behind the words

The nucleus of my vision
Translated into

The language of my expression
Will guard my rest

Until justice
Overwhelms
disappointment

Evening

At the Edge of Every Angle

Is a gentle light
Warm and hopeful
Copper-blanket bright

I thought the crown was for my head
Now I see it's for a tender word instead
Giving away
Always living this way:
Fundamentally in relationship and breaking bread
Frames and shaping the things to come
When the lights of our eyes become one
-Candles and flames-
Keeping gates and holding our names
There stand the depths: the knowledge of the Son

Before Chaos Became A Funeral

I saw the world begin
I crept between the shadows
Where the wind was tall and thin
I slipped like laughter
Between the teeth of day
I beheld the moon and fog
I heard waters sigh and play;
The crooked lines of mountains
The panting green of trees
Babbling brooks around them
Playing like children about their knees.

Before chaos was a funeral
And the world was birthed with time
I found the face of gladness
Adorned by the King of mine.

Restore

Remind the sons they are heirs
Remind the daughters they are priests
Summon them to rule
And commune in this harvest feast

Return! Take part in this Kingdom
Release your woes
And surrender your wounds
Possess the love of the Father's heart
To carry light into the graves and tombs

There were times I felt bereft of faith
Like a pauper with an empty pouch
I prayed for an old wooden stool
And I was given a cushion on the King's Couch
The shape of the world is shifting
Torment gone, oppression lifting

This deep rest

Where your eyes catch the light

Rapid movement keeping pace

Heart awake and lucid dreaming

The plans of the Father are

Laughter and surprise

Victory rises while you are sleeping

The curse is broken for the living

When with Love

We whisper

The eager vessel fills

A river rushes over

Great gates and window sills

Eyes righteous

To see the future surge to the present

The angels intently search

For the miracle of this event

Now we have the Glory of the Son

Concerning this salvation!

The grace that has come to us

Praise God for this revelation!

A Table is Prepared

Before me

While I am surrounded by so many pressures and
fears

Yet I drink a cup of joy

I eat a bowl of anger with a side of tears

Selah

My experiences are real

But viewed from the Seat of Peace

I process it all with mercy

And give my pains release

Oil burns within

Grateful praise pours from my lips

Incense lends a flavour

To the fermented wine I savour

Still waters and pastures to spare

Gathered into the cleft of a rock

So I may long linger there.

Night's Doorway to Dawn

Sunlight upon one shoulder
The cherubim-shadows resting on the other
Not really separated
But a gathering and turning

Time stands a strand
Woven into the fabric of eternity
Vouching for sands but there is no falling
Because the glass is catching
The waves of the se

Vapors from the rainbow pour into me
And up here day and night kneel before eternity
The curtains of my breath fold over
The honey-air and draw in that sweetness
Knit together in completeness
For the ragged and the weary
Be drawn into love's deep embrace

Dangerous Safety

I collected the shadows

That settled upon my fingers

Corn silk falling

Curtains of breathing light

Behind every flame

Rests space intense with murmurs

Between every blossom-apple

I find eyes while feathers wave

Hands grasping the wind

Whirlpools of ribbon-glory

Starlight and jasper

Pearls silver luminescent vapor

Breath like wine

Smile-filled teeth laughing with oil

Tomorrow was my crown I placed in the

surrounding sea

All the wheels wait for us

Wheels within wheels of dangerous safety

My Heart is a Mortar and Pestle

My worship crushed like an herb
My hope a spiced wine
I share with Wisdom
I was made to be a glass castle
filled with the sea
I throw my crown into the promise
My badges and honors into the
Misty hues of eternity

My feet lie in peace and do not wrestle
With the chaos that tries to overcome me

I pull light into my wound
and sound into my pain
I sprinkle freedom over my past
So I can be restored to me again

Psalm 91

When I hide
And disappear into His sovereign dominion
Covered by the shadow of His feathers and pinions

The sound is different
The world muffled away
Clash and bang and brash harangue
Diminished by woolen comfort
Clothed in righteousness

His voice rumbles deeper than the crust of the earth
Lower than the deep timbres of any choir
Close as the wind and warm as fire

Snares for fowls
Arrows sent from terrors in the night
I am convinced that when I am hidden
I am being given secret plans
For highest flight

Forgiveness is a catalyst
Angels protect the science of your growth
Entangle your heart in the thundering confidence
Of being wrapped in Him

O sleeper

     dream of joy

         and salvation again

Turn your face

     to the stormy skies

         That bear hope

            upon the wind

When there isn't light-

     There is lightning

         Which assails

            counterfeit truth

Awake within

     your dreams

         O sleeper

            Laugh

               for dreams are here

The end

kalah (hebrew)
Definition: to complete, finish,
accomplish, consume, or destroy

Acknowledgements

Special thanks to Amy Axby for her
dedication in editing this book.

And a whole-hearted thanks to Necia Nash,
who not only designed the beautiful cover,
but who was also instrumental in helping
me finally publish.